Father God I Wonder

Questions to help children
find their Father

ISHMAEL

Illustrated by Lynton Hemsley

KINGSWAY PUBLICATIONS

EASTBOURNE

This booklet belongs to

. . . .

ISBN 0 86065 869 4

Produced by Bookprint Creative Services
P.O. Box 827, BN21 3YJ, England for
KINGSWAY PUBLICATIONS LTD
Lottbridge Drove, Eastbourne, E. Sussex BN23 6NT
Printed in Great Britain.

Father God, who are you?

I am the person who made you and loves you more than any human person can.

But why can't I see you?

Sadly, as you are, you do evil things which hurt me. No human person can see me and still live, but you will see me one day.

When will that be?

When people die those who love me and do what Jesus says will join me in heaven.

Who is Jesus?

Jesus is my only son who came down to earth and showed my love to the people around him. He not only cared for them and healed them when they were ill, but he also taught them the way to live which would make me, their father, pleased.

Did people believe that Jesus was your son?

No they didn't. Although he was perfect and did nothing wrong, they chose to beat him and kill him rather than believe him, because they were evil.

Why didn't you stop them from killing Jesus?

I love people so much that I allowed them to do this to my only son. The only way for evil people to start a new clean life was for him to go through all this suffering. As he was dying, all the evil that has ever been done went into his perfect body, so he could take it away and destroy evil once and for all.

So is Jesus now dead with all our evil in him?

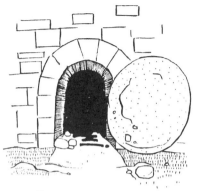

No, I told you Jesus is my son. Neither evil nor death could beat him. After three days he came back to life and in fact is with me right now.

So all my evils have been forgiven?

Yes.

Will I spend forever with you in heaven?

Well.... that depends.... you see right from the beginning I gave people a chance to choose for themselves. I didn't want to force

them to love me, so even though Jesus went through all he did, I still had to allow people to choose if they wanted to love me or not, so to show me they love me, I require them to do a few simple things.

What must I do?

1. Admit that you have done evil things like losing your temper, not telling the truth, being selfish and so on. Be really sorry for doing them. Stop doing things that just please you and begin doing the things that please me – it's not as hard as it seems because I will help you.

2. Believe that my son Jesus gave his life up because he loves you and to make you clean from all the evil you have ever done. Through his death he gives you a brand new life, he makes you a real child of mine.... you thank him.

3. The part of me who is on earth is the Holy Spirit – he's the one who is speaking to you now, even as you read this.

Invite him to come into your life and to fill you with his power, so that you can live out your life as a Christian in a way which makes me a father proud of you.

4. Spend a few moments talking to me and thanking me, because you've now done the greatest thing that can be done on earth.... You've found a real Father – you've found a real rescuer.... and you have found the Holy Spirit who, if you allow him, will help you in everything you do, every minute of the day.

Father God, what next?

If you are as excited as you should be, go and tell people you have become a Christian. Don't ever be embarrassed about me, and I won't ever be embarrassed about you.

Will life be easier now?

In some ways yes, because you now know you have me with you always, in good times and bad. But don't be surprised if there are really hard times. People will laugh at you and call you names as you try and follow me.

What else should I do?

Being with other Christians who can help and encourage you is very important, ask them to tell you about baptism and communion. You can help and encourage them too and learn together things I have taught in the Bible.

I find reading the Bible very difficult.

Don't worry – find a modern version like the Living Bible, and start reading Matthew's Gospel a little each day.

Will you help me, Father God?

Yes, of course I will.

Remember I am always with you. Don't forget to talk with me, and together we shall see many other people come to know me as their real Father, and become part of our family.

If you want to know more please contact:

I came to know God as my true
Father on

....(date)

at

....(place)